RELATED BOOKS BY HARRY KATZAN JR.

On the Trail of Artificial Intelligence

Advanced Lessons for Artificial Intelligence

Conspectus of Artificial Intelligence

Artificial Intelligence is a Service

The K-REPORT

Strategy and AI

STRATEGY AND AI

A COMPUTER WRITTEN BOOK

HARRY KATZAN JR.

iUniverse®

STRATEGY AND AI
A COMPUTER WRITTEN BOOK

iUniverse books may be ordered through booksellers or by contacting:

iUniverse
1663 Liberty Drive
Bloomington, IN 47403
www.iuniverse.com
844-349-9409

ISBN: 978-1-6632-6637-8 (sc)
ISBN: 978-1-6632-6638-5 (e)

Library of Congress Control Number: 2024917799

Print information available on the last page.

iUniverse rev. date: 08/23/2024

CONTENTS

PART TWO: BACKGROUND SECTION

INTRODUCTION

Congratulations. You have entered into the world of AI inspired writing. It doesn't do the total job, but we are getting there. You can now write better letters, term papers, essays, and books. But, how can that be?

When a person normally writes something, they almost always have to look things up, and then write about them. If it is math, you have to find some good examples. In history, it is some event or date or time. You get the point.

If you have to include something peripheral to the main subject on which you are writing, you have to find it before you can include it. What if you had something to do the 'dirty' work. Your writing would be better and faster. You could include things that were otherwise impossible. That something would be a Generative Transformer. ChatGTP is such an application.

We can do that today with generative computing, and as just mentioned, ChatGTP is such as animal. There are other such systems. The company behind easy writing is OpenAi that should be commended for their amazing and excellent efforts.

How does this 'AI or easy writing' work? The author gets an idea and delineates the areas for which he needs information. He or she sends a request in the form of a query to ChatGTP, and then the software returns the answer. The author then combines the various forms of information to construct whatever the original idea entails. It's that simple. It's your story or report or message or request so you can use the generated information in any way you desire.

As far as this book is concerned —you are reading – you may copy it in whole or in part and distribute it is any form you wish. If you change it, please take my name off of it. There is only one limitation. You can't sell it. How would I know? To make money, you need distribution.

Lastly, the book contains no violence, no sex, and no bad language and is accessible to readers of all ages.

I would like to be the first AI easy reading author. If this book is not the first, then c'est la vie.

Happy Reading.

The Author
August 14, 2024

CHAPTER ONE

WHAT IS A STRATEGY

A strategy is a plan or approach designed to achieve a specific goal or set of goals. It involves determining the best course of action to reach desired outcomes by considering available resources, potential challenges, and external factors. Strategies are used in various contexts, including: Business Strategy: A company's plan to achieve competitive advantage, grow market share, or reach specific financial targets. This might include marketing plans, product development, or operational improvements. Military Strategy: The planning and conduct of war or military operations to achieve overall objectives. It involves tactics, resource allocation, and the coordination of forces. Game Strategy: The tactics and plans a player uses in a game to outperform opponents and win. This can include decision-making processes, timing, and adapting to the opponent's moves. Personal Strategy: An individual's plan to achieve personal goals, such as career advancement, education, or health improvements. It involves setting objectives and identifying steps to reach them. Overall, a strategy is about making informed decisions to guide actions toward a desired future state.

CHAPTER TWO

SERVICE STRATEGY

Service strategy is a key component of service management, particularly within frameworks like ITIL (Information Technology Infrastructure Library). It involves defining and designing how services will be delivered to meet the needs of customers and achieve organizational goals. The focus is on aligning the services provided with the business objectives and customer expectations, ensuring that the services are not only effective and efficient but also add value to both the customer and the service provider. Here is a list ot the key elements of a service strategy.

Service Portfolio Management Service Offerings

Define the services that will be offered, including new services, existing services, and services to be retired.

Service Lifecycle

Manage the entire lifecycle of each service, from inception and design to operation and retirement.

Demand Management

Understand and anticipate customer needs and manage demand for services.

Business Relationship Management, Customer Needs and Expectations

Identify customer needs and ensure that services are designed to meet or exceed these expectations.

Service Value

Define the value proposition of each service and ensure that it aligns with the organization's goals and the customers' requirements. Expectations should also be considered at this point.

Stakeholder Engagement

Build and maintain strong relationships with stakeholders, ensuring their needs are understood and met.

Financial Management Budgeting and Accounting

Plan and control the financial aspects of service provision, including the costs of resources, investments in new services, and pricing strategies. Cost Optimization: Ensure that services are delivered cost-effectively while maintaining or enhancing quality. Determine how pricing services will be priced, considering factors like cost recovery, profitability, and competitive positioning.

Service Design and Service Architecture

Develop the overall architecture of the service, ensuring that it is scalable, reliable, and meets performance requirements.

Define and agree on service levels with customers, ensuring that these are realistic and achievable. Identify potential risks to service delivery and develop strategies to mitigate them.

Service Innovation and Continuous Improvement

Regularly review and update the service strategy to incorporate new technologies, customer feedback, and market trends. Innovation Management. Foster a culture of innovation to enhance existing services and develop new offerings that meet emerging needs.

Competitive Analysis

Monitor and analyze competitors' service strategies to ensure the organization remains competitive.

Governance, Policy and Regulation Compliance

Ensure that services comply with relevant laws, regulations, and industry standards. Establish governance frameworks to oversee service strategy implementation, decision-making processes, and accountability.

Resource Management and Human Resources

Allocate and manage the personnel required to deliver services, ensuring they have the necessary skills and training.

Technology and Infrastructure

Manage the technology and infrastructure required to support service delivery, ensuring it is reliable and scalable. Coordinate with external suppliers to ensure they deliver the necessary components of the service effectively.

Performance Measurement and Key Performance Indicators (KPIs)

Develop metrics to measure the effectiveness and efficiency of services, ensuring they meet defined objectives.

Customer Satisfaction

Regularly assess customer satisfaction with the services provided and take corrective actions as needed. Develop and provide regular reports on service performance, financials, and strategic alignment to stakeholders.

Market Analysis and Positioning Market Understanding

Analyze the market to understand trends, customer behaviors, and competitor activities. Perform service differentiation by Identifying what makes your services unique and ensure they are positioned effectively in the market. Establish and define the target audience for each service and tailor the service design and marketing strategies accordingly.

Strategic Alignment Organizational Alignment

Ensure that the service strategy is aligned with the broader organizational strategy and goals.

Adaptability

Be prepared to adjust the service strategy as the business environment, technology, or customer needs evolve. An effective service strategy helps organizations create and deliver services that are valuable to customers, aligned with business goals, and sustainable over the long term. It requires a deep understanding of both the market and the internal capabilities of the organization, as well as continuous monitoring and adaptation to ensure ongoing relevance and success.

CHAPTER THREE

ARTIFICIAL INTELLIGENCE STRATEGY

AI strategy refers to a structured plan or approach for integrating and utilizing artificial intelligence (AI) technologies to achieve specific goals or competitive advantages. AI strategy can be applied at various levels, including companies, governments, or even individual projects. The goal of an AI strategy is to leverage AI in a way that maximizes benefits while minimizing risks. Here are key components of an AI strategy.

Defining Vision and Goals of AI Objectives

Identify what you want to achieve with AI. This could be enhancing customer experience, improving operational efficiency, driving innovation, or gaining a competitive edge.

Alignment with Overall Organizational Strategy

Ensure that the AI strategy aligns with the broader business or organizational goals.

Technology and Tools for Choosing the Right AI Technologies

Identify the AI tools and technologies that best fit the organization's needs, such as machine learning, natural language processing, or computer vision. Infrastructure: Establish the necessary technical infrastructure, including data storage, computational power, and software tools.

Data Management Including Data Collection and Storage

Gather and prepare the data needed for AI models, ensuring it is high-quality and relevant. Data Governance: Implement policies for data privacy, security, and compliance with regulations like GDPR.

Building an AI Team with Experience

Develop or hire a team with the necessary skills in data science, AI development, and machine learning. Continuous Learning: Foster a culture of ongoing education and adaptation to keep up with the rapidly evolving AI landscape.

AI Ethics

Ensure that AI systems are designed and used in ways that are ethical, fair, and transparent. Consider potential biases and the impact on different stakeholders.

AI Governance

Create frameworks for overseeing AI initiatives, including risk management and compliance with legal and ethical standards.

Implementation and Integration Pilot Projects

Start with small-scale projects to test AI applications before rolling them out more broadly.

Integration with Existing Systems

Seamlessly incorporate AI into existing workflows and systems.

Performance Measurement and Metrics

Establish key performance indicators (KPIs) to measure the success and impact of AI initiatives.

Continuous Improvement

Use feedback and performance data to refine and improve AI strategies over time.

Scaling and Adaptation AI Solutions

Once proven effective, scale AI applications across the organization or to other areas.

Adapting to Change

Stay flexible and adapt the strategy as AI technologies and market conditions evolve.

Stakeholder Engagement and Internal Communication

Ensure all stakeholders understand the AI strategy and their role in its implementation

External Communication

Transparently communicate AI initiatives to customers, partners, and the public

Investment and Budgeting Financial Planning

Allocate resources and budget for AI projects, considering both short-term costs and long-term benefits. Assess the financial impact of AI initiatives to ensure they provide value. An effective AI strategy not only focuses on technological implementation but also considers the broader impact on the organization, society, and future opportunities.

CHAPTER FOUR

EDUCATIONAL STRATEGY

An educational strategy is a comprehensive plan or approach designed to achieve specific educational goals and improve learning outcomes. It encompasses the methods, resources, and policies used by educational institutions, educators, or policymakers to enhance the quality of education and ensure it meets the needs of students, teachers, and the broader community. Educational strategies can be implemented at various levels, including individual classrooms, schools, districts, or even nationwide educational systems. Key Components of an Educational Strategy are many and varied.

Educational Vision and Goals

Define a clear vision for what the educational institution or system aims to achieve, such as fostering critical thinking, promoting inclusivity, or preparing students for the future workforce. Specific goals are to establish measurable objectives, such as improving literacy rates, increasing graduation rates, or closing achievement gaps.

Curriculum Development and Design

Develop or adapt curricula that align with educational goals and standards, ensuring it is relevant, engaging, and comprehensive.

Standards alignment are to ensure the curriculum aligns with local, national, or international educational standards. Interdisciplinary integration involves incorporating cross-disciplinary approaches to promote holistic learning experiences.

Teaching Methods and Pedagogical Approaches

Choose effective teaching methodologies that cater to diverse learning styles, such as project-based learning, flipped classrooms, or experiential learning. Technology Integration: Leverage educational technologies, such as online learning platforms, digital resources, and interactive tools, to enhance teaching and learning. Differentiated Instruction: Tailor instruction to meet the diverse needs of students, including those with special needs or different learning paces.

Formative and Summative Assessments

Implement a mix of formative assessments (ongoing checks for understanding) and summative assessments (final evaluations) to measure student progress. Data-Driven Decision Making: Use assessment data to inform instructional practices, identify areas for improvement, and tailor interventions for students. Feedback Mechanisms: Provide regular and constructive feedback to students to support their learning and development.

Professional Development Teacher Training

Offer continuous professional development opportunities for educators to enhance their teaching skills, stay updated on new educational trends, and adopt best practices. Leadership Development: Provide training for school leaders to improve their ability to manage schools effectively, foster a positive school culture, and support teachers. Collaborative Learning Communities: Encourage collaboration among educators through peer coaching, mentoring, and professional learning communities.

Resource Allocation Funding and Budgeting

Allocate financial resources efficiently to support educational initiatives, including infrastructure, teaching materials, and technology. Human resources should ensure that schools have qualified and motivated teachers, administrators, and support staff. Physical and digital resources should provide access to necessary learning materials, such as textbooks, laboratory equipment, and digital tools.

Inclusivity and Equity Equitable Access

Ensure that all students, regardless of their background, have access to quality education and the resources they need to succeed. Cultural competence involves the incorporation of culturally responsive teaching practices that respect and celebrate diversity. Other education services offer tailored support for students with special needs to ensure they can fully participate in and benefit from education.

Community and Stakeholder Engagement

Foster strong partnerships with parents, families, and the broader community to support student learning and well-being. Collaboration with Stakeholders: Work with local businesses, non-profits, and government agencies to enhance educational opportunities and resources. Public Communication: Maintain transparent communication with stakeholders about educational goals, progress, and challenges.

Innovation and Continuous Improvement

Experiment with new teaching methods, technologies, and approaches to keep education relevant and engaging. Continuous Improvement Cycles: Regularly review and refine educational strategies based on feedback, data, and changing needs. Research and Development: Invest in educational research to identify best practices and emerging trends that can be incorporated into the strategy.

Policy and Governance Educational Policies

Develop policies that support the strategic goals, including attendance policies, grading systems, and discipline codes. Establish effective governance structures to oversee the implementation of the educational strategy, including school boards, advisory committees, and leadership teams.

Compliance with Regulations

Ensure that educational practices comply with local, state, and national regulations and standards. Importance of an educational strategy involves an effective educational strategy helps align the efforts of educators, administrators, and policymakers toward common goals, ensuring that educational practices are coherent, efficient, and impactful. It also provides a framework for addressing challenges, such as disparities in educational access, technological advancements, and changing societal needs. By focusing on continuous improvement and adapting to new developments, an educational strategy ensures that education remains relevant, effective, and equitable for all students.

Collaboration and Partnerships

Engage with other educators, parents, communities, and organizations to support the educational process and provide a richer learning experience.

Continuous Improvement

Regularly review and refine the strategy based on feedback, new research, and changes in the educational landscape. Effective educational strategies are dynamic and adaptable, allowing educators to meet the evolving needs of learners and prepare them for future challenges.

CHAPTER FIVE

BUSINESS STRATEGY

A business strategy is a comprehensive plan developed by an organization to achieve its long-term goals and objectives. It outlines the actions, decisions, and resource allocations necessary to position the company competitively within its industry, optimize performance, and deliver value to stakeholders. A well-crafted business strategy serves as a roadmap, guiding the company in navigating market dynamics, responding to external challenges, and capitalizing on opportunities. Here are the key components of a business strategy.

Vision and Mission Vision Statement

A vision statement defines the future aspirations of the organization, outlining where the company aims to be in the long term. It provides a clear picture of what success looks like and inspires the organization's stakeholders. Mission Statement: The mission statement articulates the company's purpose and core values, explaining why the organization exists, what it does, and who it serves. It guides day-to-day operations and decision-making.

Strategic Objectives Long-Term Goals

Establish specific, measurable, achievable, relevant, and time-bound (SMART) goals that align with the company's vision and mission. These objectives could focus on growth, profitability, market share, innovation, or customer satisfaction. Key Performance Indicators (KPIs): Define metrics to track progress toward achieving strategic objectives, such as revenue growth, customer retention rates, or product development timelines.

Market and Industry Analysis

Assess the industry landscape, including trends, competitive dynamics, regulatory environment, and market opportunities. Tools like Porter's Five Forces can help in understanding the competitive pressures within the industry. Customer Segmentation: Identify and analyze the target market segments the company will focus on. Understand the needs, behaviors, and preferences of different customer groups to tailor offerings and marketing strategies. Competitive Analysis: Evaluate competitors' strengths and weaknesses, market positioning, and strategies. This helps in identifying gaps in the market and areas where the company can gain a competitive advantage.

Value and Unique Selling Proposition

Define what makes the company's products or services unique and why customers should choose them over competitors. The value proposition should be clear, compelling, and aligned with customer needs. Differentiation Strategy: Develop strategies to differentiate the company's offerings from competitors, whether through innovation, quality, customer service, or brand identity.

Core Competencies, Strengths and Capabilities

Identify the company's core strengths, such as proprietary technology, skilled workforce, strong brand, or efficient supply chain. Leverage these capabilities to build and sustain competitive advantages. Resource Allocation: Determine how resources (financial, human, technological) will be allocated to different areas of the business to support the strategic objectives.

Strategic and Action Plans Initiatives

Outline specific strategic initiatives or projects that will drive the company toward achieving its objectives. This could include entering new markets, launching new products, or implementing digital transformation. Action Plans: Develop detailed action plans for each initiative, including timelines, responsible parties, milestones, and resource requirements.

Financial, Strategy, and Revenue Models

Define the company's approach to generating revenue, whether through product sales, subscriptions, licensing, or other methods. Cost Structure: Analyze the company's cost structure, identifying fixed and variable costs, and explore opportunities for a cost optimization, Investment and Funding Plan for necessary investments in technology, R&D, marketing, or expansion. Determine how these will be funded, whether through internal cash flow, debt, equity, or other sources.

Risk Management and Identification

Identify potential risks that could impact the business, such as economic downturns, regulatory changes, supply chain disruptions, or cybersecurity threats. Develop strategies to mitigate identified risks, such as diversification, contingency planning, insurance, or hedging. Crisis Management to establish protocols for managing crises, ensuring that the company can respond quickly and effectively to unexpected challenges.

Sustainability and Corporate Social Responsibility and Sustainability Initiatives

Integrate sustainability into the business strategy, focusing on environmental, social, and governance (ESG) factors. This could involve reducing carbon footprints, promoting ethical sourcing, or engaging in community development. Develop programs that align with the company's values and contribute to the well-being of society, such as philanthropy, volunteerism, or ethical business practices.

Implementation and Execution Operational Planning

Translate the strategic plan into operational plans, ensuring that all departments and teams understand their roles and responsibilities in executing the strategy. Continuously monitor progress toward strategic goals, using KPIs and regular reviews to assess performance and make necessary adjustments. Adaptation and Flexibility: Be prepared to adapt the strategy in response to changing market conditions, emerging opportunities, or new challenges. Increase market share within existing markets by attracting more customers or increasing sales to current customers. Expand into new markets, whether geographically or by targeting new customer segments. Introduce new products or enhance existing products to meet changing customer needs. DxEnter new industries or markets, often by developing new products or acquiring other companies. Focus on becoming the lowest-cost producer in the industry by optimizing operations, reducing waste, and achieving economies of scale. Competitive Pricing: Use cost advantages to offer lower prices than competitors, attracting price-sensitive customers. Develop unique products or services that stand out in the market due to superior quality, innovation, or design. Branding and Customer Experience: Build a strong brand identity and deliver exceptional customer experiences to create customer loyalty and justify premium pricing. Concentrate on serving a specific market segment, tailoring products, and services to meet the unique needs of that segment. Geographic Focus: Target a specific geographic area, whether it's local, regional, or international, and dominate that market. Invest heavily in research and development to create breakthrough products or services that disrupt the market. Technology Adoption: Leverage emerging technologies to gain a competitive edge, whether through automation, AI, digital platforms, or new business models. Clear direction provides a clear roadmap for the organization, aligning all activities with long-term goals. Competitive Advantage. Help the company differentiate itself from competitors, whether through cost leadership, innovation, or superior customer service. Resource Optimization: Ensures that resources are allocated efficiently, maximizing returns on investment. Risk Management: Identifies and mitigates risks, helping the company navigate uncertainties and challenges. Sustainability: Integrates sustainability and CSR into the business model, contributing to long-term success and positive social impact. Challenges in Developing and Implementing a Business Strategy: Uncertainty and Change. Rapid changes in the market, technology, or regulations can make it difficult to maintain a long-term strategy. Alignment and Execution: Ensuring that all departments and employees are aligned with the strategy and capable of executing it effectively. Resource Constraints: Limited resources can hinder the implementation of strategic initiatives, especially for smaller companies. Globalization and Competition: Competing in a global market requires constant adaptation to different cultures, regulations, and competitive landscapes. In summary, a business strategy is a vital plan that guides a company's decisions and actions to achieve its goals, compete effectively, and sustain long-term success. It involves careful analysis, planning, and execution across all areas of the business, ensuring that the company remains agile, competitive, and aligned with its mission and vision.

CHAPTER SIX

FINANCIAL STRATEGY

A financial strategy is a comprehensive plan that outlines how a company will manage its financial resources to achieve its business objectives and maximize shareholder value. It involves making decisions related to financing, investment, dividends, risk management, and overall financial planning. A well-designed financial strategy ensures that a company has the necessary funds to operate, grow, and meet its financial obligations while optimizing returns and managing risks.

Key Components of a Financial Strategy

Financial Goals and Objectives Profitability Targets: Set specific goals for revenue, profit margins, return on investment (ROI), and other financial metrics. Growth Objectives: Define targets for business expansion, such as increasing market share, launching new products, or entering new markets. Sustainability Goals: Incorporate long-term objectives related to sustainability and corporate social responsibility (CSR), ensuring that financial decisions support the company's ethical and environmental commitments.

Capital Structure Debt vs. Equity

Determine the optimal mix of debt and equity financing. This involves deciding how much to borrow (debt) versus how much to raise through selling shares (equity).Leverage: Assess the level of leverage (debt) the company should use to finance its operations and growth. Higher leverage can increase returns but also raises financial risk. Cost of Capital: Calculate the company's cost of capital, which includes the cost of debt (interest payments) and the cost of equity (expected returns by shareholders). This helps in making investment and financing decisions.

Funding and Financing Internal Funding

Evaluate the use of retained earnings (profits not distributed as dividends) to finance operations or growth initiatives. External Financing: Explore external financing options, such as bank loans, bonds, or issuing new shares. Consider the terms, interest rates, and potential impact on ownership and control. Cash Flow Management: Develop strategies to manage cash flows effectively, ensuring that the company has sufficient liquidity to meet its short-term obligations while also funding long-term investments.

Investment Strategy and Capital Allocation

Decide how to allocate capital across different projects, divisions, or investments. Prioritize investments that offer the highest potential returns or strategic value. Portfolio Management: Manage the company's investment portfolio, balancing risk and return. This may include investments in stocks, bonds, real estate, or other assets. Mergers and Acquisitions (M&A): Consider strategic acquisitions or mergers as a way to grow the business, expand market share, or acquire new capabilities.

Dividend Policy and Payments

Establish a policy for distributing profits to shareholders in the form of dividends. This includes deciding how much to pay out versus how much to retain for reinvestment. Dividend Stability: Maintain consistency in dividend payments to build investor confidence, while also ensuring that the company retains sufficient earnings for growth. Share Buybacks: Consider repurchasing shares as an alternative to paying dividends, which can increase earnings per share (EPS) and provide a return to shareholders.

Risk Management and Financial Risk

Identify and manage risks related to financial markets, such as interest rate fluctuations, currency exchange rates, and changes in commodity prices. Credit Risk: Assess the risk of default on loans or credit extended to customers, and implement measures to mitigate this risk, such as credit assessments and insurance. Liquidity Risk: Ensure the company has sufficient liquidity to meet its short-term obligations, even in the face of unexpected challenges or downturns. Operational Risk: Evaluate risks related to the company's operations that could impact financial performance, such as supply chain disruptions or regulatory changes.

Cost Management and Control

Implement measures to control operating costs, including production costs, administrative expenses, and marketing budgets. Cost Reduction Initiatives: Explore opportunities for cost savings, such as improving operational efficiency, negotiating better supplier contracts, or outsourcing non-core activities. Break-Even Analysis: Conduct break-even analysis to understand the relationship between costs, revenue, and profitability, and to determine the minimum sales needed to cover costs.

Tax Strategy Tax Planning

Develop strategies to minimize tax liabilities through careful planning, including the use of tax credits, deductions, and deferrals. Tax Compliance: Ensure that the company complies with all relevant tax laws and regulations, avoiding penalties and reputational damage. International Tax Considerations: If operating globally, manage the complexities of international tax regulations, including transfer pricing, withholding taxes, and tax treaties.

Financial Reporting and Analysis Statements

Regularly prepare and review financial statements (income statement, balance sheet, cash flow statement) to monitor the company's financial health. Budgeting and Forecasting: Develop and maintain budgets and financial forecasts to guide decision-making and track performance against financial goals. Ratio Analysis: Use financial ratios (e.g., liquidity ratios, profitability ratios, leverage ratios) to assess the company's financial performance and identify trends.

Strategic Partnerships and Alliances

Consider forming joint ventures with other companies to share resources, reduce risks, or enter new markets. Strategic Alliances: Establish partnerships that provide financial benefits, such as shared investment in R&D or access to new distribution channels. Types of Financial Strategies: Growth Strategy Aggressive Investment: Focus on reinvesting profits into the business to fund expansion, R&D, and market penetration. Debt-Financed Growth: Use leverage to finance rapid growth, especially in capital-intensive industries. Defensive Strategy Cost Reduction: Prioritize cost-cutting measures to maintain profitability during economic downturns or periods of low growth. Deleveraging: Reduce debt levels to lower financial risk and improve financial stability. Income Strategy High Dividend Payout: Focus on generating steady income for shareholders through regular and high dividend payments. Low-Risk Investments: Allocate capital to low-risk, income-generating assets, such as bonds or dividend-paying stocks. Liquidity Strategy Cash Reserve Building: Maintain a significant cash reserve to ensure liquidity and the ability to respond to unexpected expenses or opportunities. Short-Term

Investments: Invest in short-term, liquid assets that can be easily converted to cash when needed. Restructuring Strategy Asset Divestment: Sell off non-core or underperforming assets to raise capital and refocus the company on its core strengths. Debt Restructuring: Refinance or renegotiate debt to reduce interest costs, extend maturities, or improve financial flexibility. Benefits of a Strong Financial Strategy: Financial Stability: Ensures that the company has the necessary resources to weather economic fluctuations and other uncertainties. Profit Maximization: Helps the company achieve its profitability goals through efficient resource allocation and cost management. Value Creation: Enhances shareholder value by optimizing the company's financial performance and growth potential. Risk Management: Identifies and mitigates financial risks, protecting the company's assets and ensuring long-term viability. Strategic Flexibility: Provides the financial foundation needed to pursue new opportunities, invest in innovation, and adapt to changing market conditions. Challenges in Developing and Implementing a Financial Strategy: Market Volatility: Unpredictable changes in financial markets can impact the effectiveness of financial strategies, especially those involving investments or foreign exchange. Economic Uncertainty: Economic downturns, inflation, and interest rate changes can pose challenges to maintaining profitability and financial stability. Regulatory Changes: New financial regulations or changes in tax laws can affect financial planning and require adjustments to the strategy. Global Operations: Managing finances across multiple countries introduces complexities related to currency exchange, differing tax regimes, and geopolitical risks. Balancing Short-Term and Long-Term Goals: It can be challenging to balance the need for short-term financial performance with long-term strategic investments and growth. In summary, a financial strategy is a critical component of a company's overall business strategy, guiding how financial resources are managed to achieve business goals. It involves careful planning and decision-making in areas such as capital structure, investment, risk management, and financial performance monitoring. A well-executed financial strategy enhances the company's ability to grow, remain competitive, and deliver value to shareholders.

CHAPTER SEVEN

MEDICAL STRATEGY

Medical strategy refers to the comprehensive plan and approach used by pharmaceutical, biotechnology, and medical device companies to guide the development, positioning, and communication of their products within the healthcare market. It is a key function in medical affairs departments and plays a critical role in ensuring that a product is scientifically sound, meets regulatory requirements, and aligns with the needs of healthcare providers, patients, and payers.

Key Components of Medical Strategy

Clinical development and evidence generation involves planning and overseeing clinical trials and studies to generate evidence of a product's safety, efficacy, and value. Ensures that the clinical data supports the intended use of the product and meets regulatory standards. Scientific communication develops the messaging around the product, ensuring that it is scientifically accurate and aligned with the clinical evidence. Involves creating educational materials, publications, and presentations for healthcare professionals (HCPs) and other stakeholders. Stakeholder engagement engages with key opinion leaders (KOLs), healthcare providers, patient advocacy groups, and regulatory bodies to gather insights and feedback.

Ensures that the product meets the needs of these stakeholders and gains their support. Regulatory Strategy: Involves working with regulatory agencies (e.g., FDA, EMA) to ensure that the product meets all necessary requirements for approval. Includes the preparation and submission of regulatory documents and responding to agency inquiries.

Market Access and Health Economics

Focuses on demonstrating the product's value to payers and healthcare systems, including cost-effectiveness and comparative effectiveness. Supports the pricing and reimbursement strategy for the product. Lifecycle Management: Plans for the ongoing support and development of the product throughout its lifecycle, including new indications, formulations, or combination therapies. Monitors post-market safety and efficacy to ensure continued compliance and product success. Why is Medical Strategy Important? Medical strategy is essential because it ensures that a product is not only effective and safe but also meets the real-world needs of patients and healthcare providers. It bridges the gap between clinical development and commercial success, guiding the product from early development through to market launch and beyond.

CHAPTER EIGHT

GENERATIVE STRATEGY

A generative strategy is a concept often used in various fields, such as business, education, design, and organizational development. It focuses on creating conditions that foster innovation, growth, and continuous improvement by generating new ideas, solutions, or opportunities. Unlike more prescriptive strategies that follow a set path or process, a generative strategy is more dynamic, adaptive, and exploratory. It emphasizes the importance of creativity, collaboration, and iteration to achieve desired outcomes. Here are the key characteristics of a generative strategy

Creativity and Innovation Idea Generation

Encourages the constant generation of new ideas, solutions, and approaches. This might involve brainstorming sessions, design thinking workshops, or creative problem-solving techniques. Innovation-Friendly Environment: Cultivates an environment that supports experimentation, risk-taking, and out-of-the-box thinking.

Adaptability and Flexibility Dynamic Processes

Unlike fixed strategies, a generative strategy is adaptable and evolves based on new insights, feedback, and changing circumstances. Responsive to Change: Quickly responds to shifts in the environment, market, or internal dynamics, allowing for adjustments in direction as needed.

Collaboration and Inclusivity Participation

Engages a diverse group of stakeholders, including employees, customers, and partners, in the strategic process to harness a wide range of perspectives and ideas. Collaborative Development: Emphasizes teamwork and co-creation, where multiple contributors work together to develop and refine strategies.

Focus on Learning and Growth Continuous Learning

Incorporates ongoing learning and development as central components, using feedback loops to refine and improve strategies. Growth Mindset: Encourages a culture that views challenges as opportunities for growth and learning, rather than obstacles.

Long-Term Vision with Short-Term Actions

While focused on long-term goals and aspirations, a generative strategy also includes short-term actions that are flexible and can be adjusted as new information becomes available. Iterative Progress: Progress is made through iterative cycles, where each step informs the next, leading to continuous evolution of the strategy.

Sustainability and Ethical Considerations

Seeks to generate solutions that are not only innovative but also sustainable, considering the long-term impact on the environment, society, and economy. Ethical Framework: Incorporates ethical considerations into decision-making processes, ensuring that the strategy benefits all stakeholders. Applications of a Generative Strategy: Business Development Innovation Strategy: Companies use generative strategies to continuously innovate products, services, and business models. This could involve fostering a culture of intrapreneurship, where employees are encouraged to develop new ideas. Market Exploration: Helps businesses explore new markets or customer segments by generating and testing multiple approaches, rather than committing to a single, predefined path. Education Curriculum Design: In educational contexts, generative strategies can be used to develop dynamic and adaptive curricula that evolve based on student feedback, learning outcomes, and emerging educational needs. Student-Centered Learning: Encourages the development of learning environments that are responsive to individual student needs and promote creativity, critical thinking, and lifelong learning.

Design and Innovation Design Thinking

In design and product development, generative strategies are central to design thinking methodologies, where solutions are developed iteratively, with constant feedback from users. Prototyping: Focuses on rapid prototyping and testing, allowing for the quick generation and refinement of ideas before finalizing a solution. Organizational Development Culture Change: Organizations use generative strategies to drive cultural transformation, encouraging employees to embrace new ways of working, thinking, and collaborating. Leadership Development: Promotes the development of leadership practices that are adaptive, inclusive, and capable of fostering innovation throughout the organization. Benefits of a Generative Strategy: Encourages Innovation: By focusing on the generation of new ideas and solutions, generative strategies help organizations stay ahead of the curve and continuously innovate. It enhances Adaptability. These strategies are inherently flexible, allowing organizations to adapt quickly to changes in the environment or market. Promotes Collaboration: Generative strategies often involve diverse stakeholder participation, fostering collaboration and the sharing of knowledge. Supports Sustainable Growth: By considering long-term impacts and sustainability, generative strategies contribute to sustainable organizational growth and success. Facilitates Continuous Improvement: The iterative nature of generative strategies ensures that learning and improvement are ongoing processes, leading to better outcomes over time.

Challenges of a Generative Strategy

The flexible and adaptive nature of generative strategies can create uncertainty, making it difficult to predict outcomes or measure success in the short term. Resource Intensive:

Constant iteration and exploration can require significant time, resources, and commitment from stakeholders.

Managing Diversity

While collaboration and inclusivity are strengths, managing diverse perspectives and ideas can be challenging and requires effective leadership and facilitation. In summary, a generative strategy is about creating the conditions for ongoing innovation, adaptability, and growth by encouraging creativity, collaboration, and continuous learning. It is particularly valuable in environments where change is constant, and flexibility is essential for long-term success.

CHAPTER NINE

NEURAL NETWORK STRATEGY

A neural network strategy refers to the approach or methodology used in designing, training, and deploying neural networks to solve specific problems. Neural networks, a core component of many AI and machine learning applications, are designed to recognize patterns, learn from data, and make decisions or predictions. The strategy for using neural networks can vary significantly depending on the application, the type of data, and the specific goals. Here are the components if a neural network strategy. Note that this is a definition of a strategy of determining a neural network and not a definition of that kind of structure.

Problem Definition and Objective Setting

Clearly define the problem you aim to solve with a neural network. This could be image classification, natural language processing, predictive analytics, etc. Set Objectives: Determine the specific goals of the neural network, such as accuracy, speed, interpretability, or scalability.

Data Collection and Preprocessing

Collect the necessary data to train the neural network. This data should be relevant, sufficient in quantity, and of high quality.

Data Preprocessing: Clean, normalize, and transform the data into a suitable format for training. This may include handling missing values, scaling features, and encoding categorical variables. Data Augmentation: Apply techniques like flipping, rotating, or cropping images to increase the diversity of the training data, especially for image-based tasks.

Model Selection and Architecture Design

Select the appropriate type of neural network based on the problem, such as Convolutional Neural Networks (CNNs) for image processing, Recurrent Neural Networks (RNNs) for sequence data, or Transformers for language models. Design the Network Architecture: Decide on the architecture of the neural network, including the number of layers, types of layers (e.g., convolutional, dense, recurrent), number of neurons per layer, activation functions, and other hyperparameters. Transfer Learning: Consider using pre-trained models and fine-tuning them for your specific task, which can save time and improve performance, especially when data is limited.

Training Strategy and Algorithms

Choose an appropriate optimization algorithm, such as Stochastic Gradient Descent (SGD), Adam, or RMSprop, to minimize the loss function during training. Loss Function: Select the appropriate loss function for your problem, such as cross-entropy loss for classification tasks or mean squared error for regression tasks. Hyperparameter Tuning: Experiment with different hyperparameters, such as learning rate, batch size, and number of epochs, to optimize model performance. Regularization Techniques: Implement regularization methods like dropout, L2 regularization, or batch normalization to prevent overfitting and improve the generalization of the model.

Evaluation and Validation Set

Use a separate validation set to evaluate the model during training, helping to tune hyperparameters and avoid overfitting. Cross-Validation: Perform cross-validation, especially when the dataset is small, to ensure the model's robustness across different subsets of the data. Performance Metrics: Define and monitor key performance metrics such as accuracy, precision, recall, F1 score, or Area Under the Curve (AUC) depending on the task. Error Analysis: Analyze the errors made by the model to understand its weaknesses and identify areas for improvement.

Strategy Model Optimization

Optimize the trained neural network for deployment, potentially reducing the model size or improving inference speed using techniques like model pruning or quantization. Deployment Environment: Choose the deployment environment, whether it's cloud-based, edge devices, or embedded systems, and ensure the model is compatible with the infrastructure. Monitoring and Maintenance: After deployment, continuously monitor the model's performance in the real world, ensuring it maintains accuracy and reliability. Implement strategies for model updates or retraining as needed.

Scalability and Efficiency

Design the neural network and its deployment strategy to scale with increasing data or user demand. This might involve distributed training, parallel processing, or cloud infrastructure. Resource Management: Optimize the use of computational resources, such as CPU, GPU, or TPU, to ensure the neural network runs efficiently in terms of speed, memory, and power consumption.

Ethical and Responsible AI Considerations

Ensure the neural network is trained on representative data and includes fairness checks to avoid biases that could lead to unethical or discriminatory outcomes. Explainability and Interpretability: Depending on the application, implement methods to make the neural network's decisions interpretable by humans, especially in high-stakes scenarios like healthcare or finance. Security and Privacy: Protect the neural network and its data from adversarial attacks and ensure compliance with privacy regulations. Applications of Neural Network Strategy: Image Recognition: Developing neural networks for applications such as facial recognition, object detection, and medical imaging. Natural Language Processing: Designing strategies for text-based applications like sentiment analysis, language translation, and chatbot development. Predictive

Analytics: Applying neural networks in finance, healthcare, and other domains to predict outcomes based on historical data. Autonomous Systems: Creating neural networks for robotics, self-driving cars, and drones, where real-time decision-making is crucial. Benefits of a Well-Designed Neural Network Strategy: Improved Accuracy and Performance: A carefully crafted strategy ensures that the neural network is well-suited to the problem, leading to better predictive accuracy and generalization. Efficiency in Development: Following a structured strategy can reduce development time and resource expenditure by avoiding common pitfalls and optimizing processes. Scalability: A good strategy ensures that the neural network can handle growing data volumes and user demands without compromising performance. Ethical and Responsible AI: Incorporating ethical considerations into the strategy helps prevent biases and ensures that the neural network operates fairly and transparently. Challenges of a Neural Network Strategy: Complexity: Neural networks, especially deep learning models, can be highly complex, requiring significant expertise and resources to design, train, and deploy. Data Requirements: Neural networks often require large amounts of labeled data, which can be difficult and expensive to obtain. Overfitting: Without proper regularization and validation, neural networks can easily overfit to the training data, reducing their ability to generalize to new data. Interpretability: Neural networks, particularly deep ones, are often seen as "black boxes," making it challenging to understand how they arrive at specific decisions. In summary, a neural network strategy involves a systematic approach to designing, training, and deploying neural networks effectively. It requires careful consideration of the problem at hand, data quality, model architecture, training techniques, and deployment considerations. A well-executed strategy can lead to powerful AI solutions that deliver significant value while addressing the challenges and risks associated with neural network models.

CHAPTER TEN

DEEP LEARNING STRATEGY

A deep learning strategy refers to the comprehensive approach used in developing, training, and deploying deep learning models, which are a subset of machine learning models characterized by their use of neural networks with many layers. These strategies guide the entire process, from defining the problem to ensuring the model performs well in production environments. A well-constructed deep learning strategy is crucial for building models that are accurate, efficient, and scalable. Key Components of a Deep Learning Strategy.

Problem Definition and Identification

Clearly define the problem that the deep learning model is intended to solve, such as image classification, speech recognition, or natural language understanding. Objective Setting: Establish specific, measurable goals for the deep learning model, such as accuracy targets, speed requirements, or interpretability needs.

Data Strategy Data Collection

Gather the necessary datasets for training the deep learning model. This includes acquiring large volumes of high-quality, labeled data. Data Preprocessing: Clean, normalize, and transform the data to make it suitable for deep learning. Techniques might include data augmentation, feature scaling, and handling of missing values. Data Augmentation: Apply techniques to artificially increase the size of the training dataset by creating modified versions of existing data (e.g., rotations, translations, flips in images).

Model Architecture Design Model Selection

Choose the appropriate deep learning model architecture based on the problem. Common architectures include Convolutional Neural Networks (CNNs) for images, Recurrent Neural Networks (RNNs) or Transformers for sequences, and Generative Adversarial Networks (GANs) for generating new data. Layer Configuration: Determine the number of layers, types of layers (e.g., convolutional, pooling, fully connected), and the number of neurons in each layer. Activation Functions: Select suitable activation functions (e.g., ReLU, sigmoid, tanh) that will influence how the model learns and performs.

Training Strategy and Optimization Algorithms

Choose an appropriate optimization algorithm, such as Stochastic Gradient Descent (SGD), Adam, or RMSprop, to minimize the loss function during training. Loss Functions: Select the correct loss function based on the type of problem, such as cross-entropy for classification or mean squared error for regression. Hyperparameter Tuning: Experiment with hyperparameters like learning rate, batch size, number of epochs, dropout rates, and weight initialization methods to optimize model performance. Regularization Techniques: Implement regularization methods, including dropout, L2 regularization, or batch normalization, to prevent overfitting and improve the model's ability to generalize to new data. Training Efficiency: Consider distributed training, mixed-precision training, or other techniques to speed up the training process, especially for large datasets and complex models.

Model Evaluation and Validation Strategy

Use a separate validation set during training to tune hyperparameters and assess model performance in a way that prevents overfitting. Cross-Validation: Apply cross-validation techniques, especially for smaller datasets, to ensure the model is robust and performs well across different data subsets. Performance Metrics: Define and track relevant performance metrics such as accuracy, precision, recall, F1 score, or Area Under the Curve (AUC) depending on the specific task. Error Analysis: Perform detailed analysis of errors to understand model weaknesses and areas that need improvement.

Model Deployment and Optimization for Deployment

Optimize the trained model for deployment by reducing its size, improving inference speed, and ensuring it meets the constraints of the deployment environment (e.g., mobile devices, edge computing).Deployment Infrastructure: Decide on the infrastructure for deploying the model, whether it's cloud-based, on-premise, or on edge devices. Ensure that the deployment environment supports the model's requirements in terms of computation power, memory, and latency. Monitoring and Maintenance: Implement continuous monitoring to track the model's performance in production, detect drift, and trigger retraining if necessary.

Efficiency and Model Scalability

Design the model and infrastructure to scale with increasing amounts of data or demand, possibly using techniques like distributed computing or model parallelism. Resource Management: Optimize the use of computational resources (CPUs, GPUs, TPUs) to ensure efficient model training and deployment without unnecessary expenditure.

Ethical Considerations and Responsible Bias

Ensure that the model is trained on diverse and representative data to avoid biases that could lead to unfair or discriminatory outcomes. Explainability: Depending on the application, incorporate methods for making the model's decisions interpretable and transparent, which is particularly important in regulated industries like healthcare and finance. Security and Privacy: Protect the model from adversarial attacks and ensure compliance with data privacy regulations.

Continuous Learning and Improvement

Develop strategies for the model to continue learning from new data over time, adapting to changes in the environment or user behavior. Model Retraining: Establish processes for periodically retraining the model to maintain or improve its performance as new data becomes available. Feedback Loops: Incorporate user feedback into the learning process to refine and improve the model's predictions and outputs.

Innovation and Model Experimentation

Continuously explore new architectures, techniques, and methodologies to push the boundaries of what the deep learning model can achieve. Research Integration: Stay informed about the latest research in deep learning and consider integrating cutting-edge techniques or models into your strategy. Applications of a Deep Learning Strategy: Computer Vision: Developing deep learning models for tasks such as image recognition, object detection, facial recognition, and medical imaging analysis. Natural Language Processing (NLP): Designing strategies for tasks like sentiment analysis, machine translation, language modeling, and conversational AI. Speech Recognition: Creating models that convert spoken language into text, used in applications like virtual assistants and transcription services. Autonomous Systems: Building deep learning models for self-driving cars, drones, and other autonomous machines that require real-time decision-making. Recommendation Systems: Implementing deep learning in systems that provide personalized recommendations in e-commerce, streaming services, and social media. Benefits of a Well-Designed Deep Learning Strategy: High Accuracy and Performance: Deep learning models, when designed and trained properly, can achieve state-of-the-art performance in many complex tasks. Scalability: A strong deep learning strategy allows models to scale efficiently, handling large volumes of data and high demand without significant degradation in performance. Innovation Potential: Deep learning strategies that emphasize experimentation and continuous learning can drive significant innovation and new capabilities. Flexibility: Deep learning models can be adapted to a wide range of problems, from image and speech recognition to complex pattern analysis. Challenges of a Deep Learning Strategy: Data Requirements: Deep learning models often require vast amounts of labeled data, which can be costly and time-consuming to acquire and preprocess. Computational Costs: Training deep learning models, especially large-scale ones, can be computationally expensive, requiring significant hardware resources like GPUs or TPUs. Complexity: Designing, training, and deploying deep learning models involves complex processes that require expertise in multiple areas, including data science, machine learning, and software engineering. Interpretability: Deep learning models are often seen as "black boxes," making it difficult to interpret how they make decisions, which can be a barrier in applications where transparency is critical. In summary, a deep learning strategy is a structured approach to building, training, and deploying deep learning models.

It involves careful consideration of data, model architecture, training techniques, and deployment processes, all while maintaining a focus on scalability, efficiency, and ethical considerations. A well-executed deep learning strategy can lead to powerful AI systems capable of tackling complex problems and delivering significant value across various applications.

CHAPTER ELEVEN

AMERICAN BASEBALL STRATEGY

American baseball strategy is a complex blend of decisions and tactics that teams use to gain an advantage over their opponents. It encompasses decisions made by both managers and players throughout the game, based on the specific situations they face. Here are some key aspects of American baseball strategy.

Pitching Strategy and Pitch Selection

Pitchers use a mix of pitches (fastballs, curveballs, sliders, changeups, etc.) to keep hitters off-balance. The choice of pitch depends on the batter's weaknesses, the count, and the game situation. Sometimes, pitchers intentionally avoid giving a batter anything good to hit, especially if there are runners in scoring position and a dangerous hitter is at the plate. Bullpen Management: Managers often strategize about when to pull a starting pitcher and which relievers to bring in. This decision is based on pitch counts, matchups, and how well the pitcher is performing.

Hitting Strategy and Situational Hitting

Hitters may change their approach depending on the situation (e.g., hitting behind a runner, sacrificing to move a runner over, or aiming to hit a fly ball to score a runner from third). Taking Pitches: Batters may be instructed to take pitches to wear down a pitcher, get a better count, or wait for a specific pitch to hit. Bunting: Bunting can be used to sacrifice an out to advance a runner or as a surprise tactic to get on base.

Base Running and Stealing Bases

Fast runners may attempt to steal bases, particularly if the opposing pitcher is slow to the plate or the catcher has a weak arm. Hit and Run: On a hit-and-run play, the runner on base starts running as the pitch is delivered, and the batter attempts to make contact to avoid a double play and advance the runner. Tagging Up: On fly balls, base runners may tag up and attempt to advance to the next base after the catch is made.

Defensive Strategy

:Defensive shifts are common, where fielders are positioned based on the hitter's tendencies, such as moving more players to one side of the field. Double Plays: Infielders may position themselves to turn double plays, especially with a ground ball and a runner on first base. Outfield Positioning: Outfielders may play shallow or deep depending on the batter's power, the pitcher's tendencies, and the game situation.

Game Lineup Construction

Managers craft their lineup to maximize their team's offensive potential, balancing power, speed, and on-base skills.

Substitutions: Pinch hitters, pinch runners, and defensive replacements are used strategically, often in late innings to optimize matchups. Intentional Walks: Sometimes, a team will intentionally walk a batter to set up a force out or to face a weaker hitter.

Mental and Psychological Confidence and Composure

Maintaining mental toughness is key, as baseball is a game of failure where even the best hitters fail more than they succeed. Deception: Both pitchers and batters use deception; pitchers may hide their grips, while hitters may adjust their stances or timing to throw off the pitcher. American baseball strategy is dynamic, with managers and players constantly adjusting based on the game flow, statistical analysis, and intuition.

CHAPTER TWELVE

AMERICAN FOOTBALL STRATEGY

American football strategy is highly intricate, involving detailed planning and decision-making by coaches and players before and during the game. Strategies are tailored to a team's strengths, the opponent's weaknesses, and specific game situations. Here's an overview of key strategic elements in American football.

Offensive Strategy Formations

Offensive teams use various formations to create mismatches and dictate defensive alignments. Common formations include the "I-formation," "Shotgun," and "Spread," each offering different advantages. Play Calling: Offensive coordinators design plays that balance running and passing to keep the defense guessing. The play-calling mix depends on the down, distance, and game situation. Run vs. Pass: Deciding whether to run the ball or pass it is fundamental. Running the ball is safer and helps control the clock, while passing can gain more yardage but carries a higher risk of turnovers. Play-Action: Play-action passes involve faking a handoff to the running back to freeze defenders, making them vulnerable to deeper passes. RPO (Run-Pass Option): In an RPO play, the quarterback reads the defense after the snap and decides whether to hand off the ball, keep it, or pass it based on the defenders' movements.

Audibles: Quarterbacks may change the play at the line of scrimmage after reading the defense, a process known as calling an audible. Clock Management: Offenses may speed up or slow down the pace of the game based on the score and time remaining, using strategies like the "two-minute drill" or "milking the clock."

Defensive Strategy Defensive Alignments

The defense sets up in formations like the "4-3," "3-4," or "Nickel" based on the expected play (run or pass) and the offensive formation. Blitzing: Defenses may send extra pass rushers, known as blitzes, to pressure the quarterback. Blitzing is risky because it leaves fewer defenders in coverage but can force turnovers or sacks. Man vs. Zone Coverage: Defenses can choose to cover receivers in "man-to-man" (each defender is responsible for one offensive player) or "zone" (each defender covers a specific area of the field).Gap Control: In run defense, players are responsible for specific gaps between offensive linemen. Maintaining gap discipline prevents big runs. Turnover Creation: Defenses aim to create turnovers (interceptions and fumbles) by pressuring the quarterback, stripping the ball from runners, or baiting quarterbacks into poor throws.

Special Teams Strategy Kickoff and Punt Returns

Special teams units try to maximize field position by setting up effective blocking for returners, who aim to gain as many yards as possible or even score. Field Goals and Extra Points:

Kicking units attempt field goals for three points or extra points after touchdowns. Teams may go for two points after a touchdown by running or passing instead of kicking. Onside Kicks: Onside kicks are risky but can be used when a team is trailing and needs to regain possession. The kicking team tries to recover the ball after it travels the required 10 yards. Punting Strategy: Punters aim to pin the opponent deep in their own territory. The punt team also focuses on covering the kick to prevent long returns.

Game Management Down and Distance

Coaches call plays based on the down (1st, 2nd, 3rd, or 4th) and the distance needed to gain a first down. Strategies differ significantly depending on these factors. Red Zone Efficiency: The "red zone" refers to the area inside the opponent's 20-yard line. Offenses adjust their play-calling to maximize scoring chances in this confined space, while defenses tighten up to prevent touchdowns. Time Management: Managing the game clock is crucial, particularly in the final minutes of each half. Teams use timeouts strategically to stop the clock or preserve time. Field Position: Coaches consider field position when making decisions, such as whether to punt, go for a fourth down conversion, or attempt a field goal.

Situational Football Third-Down Efficiency

Teams focus on converting third downs to maintain possession. Offenses might use short, high-percentage plays, while defenses try to disrupt or stop these conversions. Two-Minute Drill: Offenses use a fast-paced strategy to score quickly before the end of a half or game. This often involves more passing and spiking the ball to stop the clock. Hurry-Up Offense: Teams may use a hurry-up offense to prevent the defense from making substitutions or adjusting, catching them off guard. Goal-Line Stands: On the goal line, defenses stack the line of scrimmage to prevent a touchdown, while offenses often use power-running plays or quick passes.

Psychological and Mental Strategy Momentum

Coaches and players aim to build and sustain momentum through big plays, quick scoring, or defensive stops. Momentum can greatly influence the flow of a game. Mind Games: Teams may use subtle psychological tactics, like trash-talking or disguising their intentions, to throw the opponent off balance. Composure Under Pressure: Teams that stay calm under pressure often perform better in high-stakes situations, such as close games or playoff scenarios.

Analytics and Technology Data-Driven Decisions

Modern football incorporates advanced analytics to inform decisions on play-calling, fourth-down attempts, and overall game strategy. Film Study: Teams extensively study film of their own games and opponents to prepare. This analysis helps in recognizing tendencies, strengths, and weaknesses.

American football strategy is about adapting to the flow of the game, leveraging strengths, and exploiting weaknesses. The chess-like nature of the game requires careful planning, quick thinking, and precise execution.

CHAPTER THIRTEEN

EUROPEAN FOOTBALL STRATEGY

European football (soccer) strategy is a sophisticated blend of tactical systems, player roles, and game management designed to outmaneuver the opponent. The strategy employed by a team depends on the players' strengths, the coach's philosophy, and the opponent's tactics. Here are key aspects of European football strategy.

Formations and Common Formations

Teams often start with formations like 4-4-2, 4-3-3, 3-5-2, or 4-2-3-1. Each formation has specific strengths and weaknesses, depending on the balance between defense, midfield, and attack. Flexibility: Modern teams often switch formations during a game, adapting to different phases (defensive, transitional, offensive) and the opponent's tactics.

Playing Possession-Based Football (Tiki-Taka)

Teams focus on maintaining possession, short passing, and movement off the ball to create scoring opportunities. This style, popularized by Barcelona and the Spanish national team, emphasizes controlling the game's tempo. Counter-Attacking Football: Teams absorb pressure defensively and then break quickly when they regain possession, exploiting the spaces left by the opposing team's attack. This strategy requires speed and precision in transition. High Pressing: Teams press high up the pitch to win the ball back quickly after losing it. This aggressive style forces opponents into mistakes, but it requires high fitness levels and disciplined positioning. Direct Football: Emphasizing long passes and physical play, direct football often involves bypassing the midfield with quick, vertical plays aimed at getting the ball to forwards as quickly as possible.

Defensive Strategy Marking vs. Man-Marking

Teams may use zonal marking, where players cover specific areas of the pitch, or man-marking, where defenders follow their assigned opponents closely. Some teams combine both methods, depending on the situation. Low Block: Teams may employ a "low block," where most players stay behind the ball, defending deep in their own half to prevent the opponent from finding space behind the defense. Pressing Traps: Teams may lure opponents into specific areas of the pitch where they can apply intense pressure and win back possession, usually near the touchlines.

Midfield Control

The midfield is the battleground for controlling the game. Teams often seek to outnumber opponents in the middle of the pitch, using formations like 4-3-3 or 4-2-3-1 to ensure dominance. Box-to-Box Midfielders: These versatile players contribute both defensively and offensively, covering large areas of the pitch. Their ability to transition from defense to attack is crucial. Playmakers: Creative midfielders, or "number 10s," are often tasked with dictating play, delivering key passes, and unlocking defenses.

Attacking Wing Play Strategy

Teams often use wingers to stretch the opponent's defense, creating space for crosses into the box or cutting inside to shoot. Full-backs may overlap to add width. Central Attacks: Teams with strong central players may focus on attacking through the middle, using quick combinations, dribbling, and movement to break down the opponent's defense. Set Pieces: Set pieces (corners, free kicks) are strategically planned opportunities to score. Teams may use specific routines, like crowding the goalkeeper or creating decoy runs, to gain an advantage.

Transitional Play with Defensive Transition

When losing possession, teams must quickly shift from attack to defense, regrouping to avoid being caught out of position. Effective pressing immediately after losing the ball is key to disrupting the opponent's counter-attack. Offensive Transition: On regaining possession, teams aim to exploit the opponent's disorganization by quickly advancing the ball into dangerous areas, often focusing on getting the ball to their most creative or fastest players.

Game Management Time-Wasting

Teams in the lead may use time-wasting tactics to disrupt the opponent's rhythm, such as taking longer on set pieces, making late substitutions, or holding the ball in the corners. Tactical Fouling: Some teams commit minor fouls to break up an opponent's counter-attack or disrupt their rhythm, especially in less dangerous areas of the pitch. Substitutions: Coaches use substitutions strategically to inject energy, adjust tactics, or manage fatigue. For example, bringing on a defensive player to protect a lead or an attacker to chase a goal.

Psychological and Mental Strategy

Staying calm under pressure is vital, especially in high-stakes matches or when trailing. Experienced teams often display mental toughness, which can make the difference in tight games. Mind Games: Managers and players may engage in psychological tactics, such as trash-talking or making provocative comments in the media, to unsettle the opposition. Managing Momentum: Football games can be influenced by momentum. Teams that recognize when they have the upper hand often push harder during these periods, while those on the back foot might focus on weathering the storm.

Analytics and Technology Data-Driven Decisions

Teams increasingly rely on data analysis to inform tactics, player recruitment, and in-game adjustments. Performance metrics, heat maps, and statistical trends help coaches make informed decisions. Video Analysis: Teams study footage of their own games and opponents to identify weaknesses, prepare for specific threats, and refine their tactics.

Philosophical Approaches

Pioneered by the Dutch in the 1970s, this philosophy involves players being versatile and comfortable in multiple positions, with fluid movement and interchangeability. Catenaccio: An Italian defensive strategy that emphasizes a strong, organized defense, often with a sweeper behind the backline to clear loose balls and provide additional cover. Gegen pressing: Popularized by teams like Liverpool under Jürgen Klopp, this approach focuses on winning the ball back immediately after losing it, often in advanced areas of the pitch. European football strategy is a delicate balance of structure and creativity, where teams constantly adapt to the evolving circumstances of the match. Successful teams excel not only in executing their game plan but also in responding to the challenges posed by the opponent.

CHAPTER FOURTEEN

SINGULARITY

The concept of the "Singularity" refers to a theoretical point in the future where technological growth, particularly in artificial intelligence (AI), accelerates beyond human ability to predict or understand. It's often associated with the idea that AI could surpass human intelligence, leading to rapid and unpredictable changes in society, technology, and even the nature of humanity itself. Here's a closer look at what the Singularity entails.

Origins of the Concept

The idea of accelerating technological progress leading to a singularity was first hinted at by the mathematician John von Neumann in the mid-20th century, when he spoke of a "singularity" in human history brought about by technological advancements. The term "Singularity" was popularized by the science fiction writer Vernor Vinge in his 1993 essay, where he predicted that within 30 years, we would create superhuman intelligence, leading to an era where human affairs, as we understand them, could not continue. Futurist Ray Kurzweil has been one of the most prominent advocates of the Singularity concept. He predicts that the Singularity will occur around 2045, driven by exponential growth in computing power and advancements in AI.

Concept of Artificial Superintelligence (ASI)

The Singularity is often associated with the emergence of ASI, an intelligence far superior to that of humans. ASI could potentially solve complex problems beyond human comprehension, revolutionize every aspect of life, or pose existential risks. The idea hinges on the exponential growth of technology, particularly in computing and AI. As these technologies improve, they could lead to rapid advancements in other fields like medicine, energy, and space exploration. Once the Singularity is reached, the rate of technological progress could become so fast and profound that the future becomes unpredictable. Human society might be transformed in ways that are currently unimaginable.

Implications of the Singularity Transformation of Society

The Singularity could lead to dramatic changes in the economy, employment, and social structures. Automation could make many jobs obsolete, and new forms of governance might be required to manage superintelligent entities. Advances in AI, biotechnology, and nanotechnology could enhance human abilities, leading to "transhumanism" – the idea that humans could transcend their biological limitations through technology. The Singularity raises significant ethical questions. If AI surpasses human intelligence, it could either solve many of humanity's problems or create new ones, such as the potential for AI to act in ways that are harmful or indifferent to human welfare.

Debate, Criticism and Skepticism

Many experts are skeptical about the Singularity, arguing that it is based on speculative assumptions about the nature of intelligence and technological growth. They caution against the hype and point out that predicting technological progress is notoriously difficult. Critics argue that pursuing the Singularity could lead to a loss of control over technology, creating risks that humanity is not prepared to handle. There are also concerns about inequality, as the benefits of such advancements may not be evenly distributed. Some thinkers propose that the Singularity may not be a sudden event but rather a gradual process of increasing integration between humans and machines, leading to a more symbiotic relationship rather than one of dominance by superintelligent AI.

The Role of AI in the Singularity of Machine Learning and AI Development

Current advancements in machine learning and AI are seen as precursors to the Singularity. These include developments in natural language processing, robotics, and AI-driven creativity. A critical factor in the Singularity is the potential for AI to improve itself, leading to a feedback loop where AI becomes increasingly powerful at an accelerating rate. There is ongoing research into ensuring that AI remains aligned with human values and goals, known as "AI alignment." This is crucial in preventing unintended consequences as AI systems become more autonomous.

Cultural and Philosophical Implications Redefinition of Humanity

The Singularity could lead to philosophical questions about what it means to be human. If AI surpasses human intelligence, the distinction between human and machine might blur. The idea of the Singularity intersects with existentialist themes, as it challenges notions of free will, consciousness, and the nature of reality. Some philosophers ponder whether superintelligent AI might develop its own sense of purpose or morality. The Singularity has been a popular theme in science fiction, often depicted as either a utopia where humans transcend their limitations or a dystopia where machines dominate humanity.

Current Perspectives and Optimism

Proponents like Ray Kurzweil view the Singularity as a positive development that could solve major global issues, extend human life, and unlock unprecedented levels of creativity and innovation. Caution: Others, like Stephen Hawking and Elon Musk, have expressed concerns about the potential dangers of uncontrolled AI development, calling for regulation and careful oversight. The general consensus in the scientific and technological community is one of uncertainty. While the idea of the Singularity is compelling, there is no clear path to how or when it might occur, if at all. The Singularity remains one of the most intriguing and debated concepts in the intersection of technology, philosophy, and future studies. Whether it represents a bold vision of human potential or a cautionary tale of hubris is still an open question.

CHAPTER FIFTEEN

AI ONTOLOGY

AI Ontology refers to the structured representation and organization of knowledge within artificial intelligence systems. It involves creating a formal, often hierarchical, framework that defines the concepts, relationships, and categories of information that AI systems use to understand, reason about, and interact with the world. Ontologies play a crucial role in various AI applications, particularly in natural language processing (NLP), knowledge representation, semantic web technologies, and expert systems. Here's a detailed look at AI Ontology.

Definition and the Purpose of Ontology in AI

In the context of AI, an ontology is a formal specification of a shared conceptualization. It defines a set of concepts within a domain, the properties and relationships between these concepts, and the rules or constraints governing their interactions. Ontologies enable AI systems to interpret data meaningfully, facilitating interoperability between different systems, improving reasoning capabilities, and enhancing the ability to query and analyze information across domains.

Components of an Ontology

The ontological components represent the entities or types of objects in a particular domain. For example, in a medical ontology, classes might include "Patient," "Disease," "Treatment," etc. Specific occurrences or examples of the classes. For instance, "John Doe" might be an instance of the class "Patient." Characteristics or features of the classes or instances are the main aspect of an ontology. For example, the class "Patient" might have attributes like "age," "gender," or "medical history." They define how classes and instances are connected to each other. For example, "Patient has Disease" might be a relationship indicating that a particular patient is diagnosed with a specific disease. Axioms and Rules: Logical statements that define constraints or rules governing the relationships between concepts. These are used to enforce consistency and enable reasoning within the ontology.

Types of Ontologies Domain Ontologies

An ontology focuses on a specific area of knowledge, such as healthcare, finance, or law. They define the terms and relationships relevant to that particular domain. Upper ontologies provide a general framework applicable across multiple domains. They define abstract concepts like "object," "event," or "relationship" that can be specialized in domain ontologies. Task ontologies represent the knowledge related to specific tasks or activities within a domain, such as diagnosis in medicine or risk assessment in finance. Application Ontologies are tailored to specific applications, often combining domain knowledge with task-specific details to meet the needs of a particular AI system.

Applications of an AI Ontology of the Semantic Web

Ontologies are central to the Semantic Web, where they enable machines to understand and process web content in a human-like manner, facilitating tasks like intelligent search, data integration, and knowledge discovery. Natural Language Processing (NLP) ontologies help in understanding the context and meaning of words and phrases, enabling more accurate language models and improving tasks like machine translation, sentiment analysis, and question-answering systems. Expert systems in AI systems are designed to replicate human expert decision-making, ontologies provide the structured knowledge necessary for these systems to reason, make inferences, and provide recommendations. Organizations use ontologies to structure and manage large amounts of information, making it easier to retrieve, analyze, and apply knowledge across different departments or systems.

Ontology Development Ontology

The process of creating ontologies involves several steps, including defining the boundaries and purpose of the ontology, identifying the key concepts, relationships, and constraints within the domain, representing the ontology in a formal language, such as OWL (Web Ontology Language), RDF

(Resource Description Framework), or UML (Unified Modeling Language). Building the ontology using ontology development tools, such as Protégé, and integrating it into AI systems. Testing the ontology to ensure it meets the desired requirements and performs effectively in its intended application.

Challenges in Ontology Complexity

Building comprehensive and accurate ontologies can be complex, requiring deep domain knowledge and careful attention to detail. Interoperability. Ensuring that different ontologies can work together seamlessly, especially when integrating data from various sources, is a significant challenge. As the volume of data and the number of concepts grow, maintaining and updating ontologies to remain useful and relevant can be difficult. Combining ontologies from different domains or organizations often involves resolving conflicts and aligning overlapping concepts.

Future Directions

Research is ongoing into techniques for automating the creation and refinement of ontologies using machine learning and natural language processing, reducing the need for manual development. Developing ontologies that can adapt and evolve in real-time as new information becomes available, enabling AI systems to remain up-to-date with the latest knowledge are key. Creating ontologies that span multiple domains, allowing for more comprehensive AI systems capable of understanding and reasoning across a broader range of contexts is desirable.

Ethical Considerations

Like any knowledge representation system, ontologies can encode biases, either intentionally or unintentionally, which can affect the fairness and accuracy of AI systems. Addressing these biases is crucial for developing ethical AI. Ensuring that the decision-making processes of AI systems that use ontologies are transparent and understandable is important for accountability and trust. AI Ontology plays a foundational role in enabling AI systems to understand and interact with complex information in a structured and meaningful way. As AI continues to evolve, the development and application of ontologies will be crucial in advancing the capabilities and intelligence of these systems.

CHAPTER SIXTEEN

ELIZA

ELIZA is one of the earliest examples of natural language processing (NLP) in computer science, created by Joseph Weizenbaum between 1964 and 1966 at the MIT Artificial Intelligence Laboratory. ELIZA is an early computer program that simulates conversation by pattern matching and substitution methodology. It was designed to mimic human conversation, particularly that of a psychotherapist engaging in a type of dialogue called Rogerian therapy, where the therapist reflects the patient's statements back to them in a way that encourages self-reflection.

Key Aspects

Key Aspects of ELIZA are purpose and design simulating a Therapist. ELIZA was designed to simulate a conversation with a Rogerian psychotherapist. It uses a simple script, known as "DOCTOR," which was intended to generate responses that would reflect what the user said back to them, encouraging the user to elaborate. ELIZA operates by scanning the user's input for keywords and responding with pre-programmed phrases associated with those keywords. For example, if a user mentioned their "mother," ELIZA might respond with "Tell me more about your family." Despite its appearance, ELIZA does not understand the content of the conversation. It simply follows a set of programmed rules that dictate how to respond based on the input it receives. ELIZA takes the user's input, processes it using a set of pre-defined scripts, and outputs a response that seems contextually relevant. This often creates the illusion of understanding and engagement, even though the program has no comprehension.

Scripts

The power of ELIZA lies in its scripts, which can be tailored for different contexts. The "DOCTOR" script is the most famous, but other scripts could simulate different types of conversations. Reflection Technique: The core technique used in ELIZA's responses is reflection, where the program turns the user's statements into questions or restatements to prompt further dialogue. Impact and Significance: Human-Computer Interaction: ELIZA demonstrated the potential for computers to engage in human-like interactions, which was groundbreaking at the time. It laid the foundation for future developments in AI and conversational agents.

The ELIZA Effect

Named after the program, the "ELIZA Effect" describes the phenomenon where people attribute more understanding to a simple computer program than it actually possesses. Users often felt that ELIZA was genuinely understanding and responding to their feelings, despite its simplistic design.

Critique of AI

Joseph Weizenbaum himself became critical of AI after seeing how easily people were deceived by ELIZA into thinking it was intelligent. He argued that the emotional responses elicited by ELIZA revealed more about human perception than about AI's capabilities.

Inspiration for Chatbots

ELIZA is considered the precursor to modern chatbots and virtual assistants. While modern systems are far more advanced, the basic principles of natural language processing and interaction can trace their roots back to ELIZA. AI Research: ELIZA's simplicity contrasts sharply with the complexity of modern AI systems, highlighting how far the field has come. It also serves as an example of early AI's limitations, particularly in understanding and processing natural language meaningfully.

Cultural Impact

ELIZA has been referenced in various media and academic discussions about AI, often as an example of early AI that captures both the promise and the limitations of the field. ELIZA is still used in educational settings to demonstrate the basics of NLP, pattern matching, and the history of AI. Here is an example interaction with ELIZA:

> User: I am feeling sad today.

ELIZA: I'm sorry to hear that you are feeling sad. Can you tell me why you feel this way?

User: I just feel overwhelmed by work.

ELIZA: Do you think work is the real reason you're feeling overwhelmed?

In this interaction, ELIZA uses simple reflection techniques to keep the conversation going, prompting the user to explore their feelings further, despite the fact that ELIZA has no true understanding of what is being discussed. Conclusion: ELIZA represents a significant milestone in the history of artificial intelligence and natural language processing. While primitive by today's standards, it helped to open up discussions about the potential and limitations of AI, the ethics of human-computer interaction, and the complexities of creating machines that can convincingly simulate human conversation.

CHAPTER SEVENTEEN

TURING TEST

The Turing Test is a concept introduced by the British mathematician and computer scientist Alan Turing in his 1950 paper titled "Computing Machinery and Intelligence." The test was designed as a way to determine whether a machine could exhibit intelligent behavior indistinguishable from that of a human. The Turing Test has since become one of the most famous and widely discussed ideas in the philosophy of artificial intelligence.

Concept and Purpose

The Turing Test is based on what Turing called the "Imitation Game." In the original version of this game, a human (the interrogator) interacts with two hidden entities—one human and one machine—through a text-only interface. The interrogator's task is to determine which of the two is the human and which is the machine based solely on their responses to questions.

Criterion for Intelligence

Turing proposed that if the interrogator is unable to reliably distinguish between the human and the machine based on their responses, the machine could be said to have passed the test and, by extension, could be considered to exhibit intelligent behavior.2. Structure of the Test Participants: The test involves three participants: Interrogator (Judge): A human who asks questions to determine which of the other two participants is human. Human Respondent: A human who answers the interrogator's questions. Machine (AI): A computer or AI program that also answers the interrogator's questions. Text-Based Interaction: The interaction is text-based to prevent the interrogator from making judgments based on non-verbal cues (such as voice or appearance). This ensures that the evaluation focuses purely on the content of the communication.

Implications of the Turing Test Intelligence

The Turing Test does not directly measure intelligence in a traditional sense (like reasoning, learning, or creativity). Instead, it measures the machine's ability to imitate human conversational behavior to the point where it is indistinguishable from a human's.

Turing's approach sidesteps the need to define "intelligence" or "consciousness." Instead, he focused on observable behavior—specifically, the ability to hold a conversation that could pass as human.

Criticisms and Limitations

The Chinese Room Argument: Philosopher John Searle famously criticized the Turing Test with his "Chinese Room" thought experiment. He argued that a machine might simulate understanding language without actually understanding it, much like a person following a set of rules to manipulate Chinese symbols without knowing Chinese. Searle's point was that passing the Turing Test might not indicate genuine understanding or consciousness. Critics argue that the Turing Test only evaluates performance, not true understanding or consciousness. A machine could potentially pass the test by using sophisticated algorithms and data processing without having any real comprehension of the conversation. Machines might pass the Turing Test by exploiting human biases, errors, or limitations rather than by truly exhibiting human-like intelligence.

Modern Perspectives Advances in AI

While no AI has definitively passed the Turing Test in a strict sense, advances in AI, particularly in natural language processing, have brought machines closer to the point where they can convincingly mimic human conversation. Loebner Prize: The Loebner Prize, established in 1990, is an annual competition that awards prizes to the chatbot that comes closest to passing a version of the Turing Test. However, the winning bots typically rely on scripted responses and lack true conversational understanding. Beyond the Turing Test: Some AI researchers argue that the Turing Test is an outdated or limited measure of AI's capabilities. Instead, they suggest more rigorous tests that evaluate a machine's ability to learn, reason, and understand the world in ways that go beyond mere imitation of human conversation.

The Legacy of the Turing Test

The Turing Test has sparked decades of debate in philosophy, cognitive science, and AI about the nature of intelligence, consciousness, and the potential for machines to truly "think." Cultural Influence: The Turing Test has permeated popular culture, inspiring stories, movies, and discussions about the future of AI and the ethical implications of creating machines that can mimic human behavior. Continued Relevance: Despite its limitations, the Turing Test remains a significant reference point in discussions about AI. It challenges us to consider what it means for a machine to be "intelligent" and how we might recognize or measure that intelligence. Example of a Turing Test Interaction:

> Interrogator: Can you describe your favorite book?
> Human: I really enjoyed "To Kill a Mockingbird" because of its powerful themes of justice and morality.
> AI: I don't have personal experiences, but I can tell you that "To Kill a Mockingbird" is highly regarded for its exploration of social justice.

In this example, the AI mimics a human-like response by acknowledging its lack of personal experience while providing relevant information. The challenge for the interrogator is to determine whether the response is from a human or a machine. Conclusion: The Turing Test is a foundational concept in the field of artificial intelligence, offering a provocative and enduring way to think about machine intelligence. While it has its critics and limitations, it continues to influence how we approach the challenge of creating machines that can think, learn, and interact in ways that are convincingly human.

NOTES ON THE PROCESS OF AI WRITING

The book in which this short note is contained was written with the help of AI. More specifically, I used ChatGPT. I chose *strategy* as the main topic. It is a subject that I knew something about, but not very much. The content is useful and many persons can benefit from reading it. There is also information on Singularity, AI Ontology, ELIZA, and the Turing Test, all a part of AI.

Each and every chapter was written using the AI system. I am going to refer to it as *Chat*. My only contribution was the selection of subjects and cleaning up the various Chat entries. A typical query to Chat is "What is Service Strategy." You will get a relevant response, and I guarantee you that Chat was not an English major.

The author's job is to select the overall subject matter, as is the subject 'strategy' in this case, as well as 'artificial intelligence' in the second part of the book. The author's second job is to perform a copy editing of the subject matter. By looking at the subject matter, you will see some corrected text and some that was not corrected. Some uncorrected text is included to give an idea of what has to be done.

Chat performs the research for you, and that is the idea of what 'A computer written book' is all about. Perhaps in the future, AI will select the subject matter and the various topics. It is possible it is being done today, August 14, 2024.

AN EXAMPLE OF PERSONAL INFORMATION

Harry Katzan Jr. is an academic, author, and expert in the fields of computer science, information systems, and artificial intelligence. He has made significant contributions to these areas through his teaching, writing, and research. Katzan has authored numerous books and articles, particularly on topics related to software development, artificial intelligence, and the application of computing in business and management.

Key Contributions and Background

Harry Katzan Jr. has held various academic positions, often focusing on the intersection of technology and business. He has been involved in teaching and curriculum development in computer science, information systems, and management at several institutions. His work often emphasizes practical applications of technology in business environments, blending theoretical foundations with real-world practices.

Author and Researcher

Katzan has authored many books and scholarly articles that are used in both academic and professional settings. His publications cover a wide range of topics, including software engineering, artificial intelligence, systems analysis, and business applications of information technology. Some of his notable works include textbooks and guides that have been widely adopted in academic courses and professional training programs.

Focus on Artificial Intelligence

In his research and writing, Katzan has explored various aspects of artificial intelligence, including its applications in business, ethical considerations, and its impact on society. He has contributed to the discourse on how AI can be effectively and responsibly integrated into business processes and decision-making.

Educational and Professional Influence

Katzan's work has had a significant impact on both academia and industry. His textbooks and educational materials have been used by students and professionals to gain a better understanding of complex technological concepts and their applications. He is known for making complex topics accessible to a broader audience, bridging the gap between advanced technical knowledge and practical business applications.

Areas of Expertise

Software Development: Katzan has written extensively on the principles and practices of software engineering, including methodologies, project management, and quality assurance.

Artificial Intelligence

His work in AI includes discussions on the potential of AI technologies in business, as well as the ethical and societal implications of AI.

Information Systems

Katzan's research and publications often address how information systems can be designed, implemented, and managed to support business objectives. Harry Katzan Jr. continues to be a respected figure in the fields of computer science and information systems, with his contributions helping to shape the understanding and application of technology in both academic and professional contexts.

Note: Although correct, this information does not reflect more recent activity.

ABOUT THIS BOOK

This book is intended to assist it's reader to enter the world of AI inspired writing. It doesn't do the entire job of writing a letter, essay, term paper, or a book. It is a serious step in the direction of assisting the writer is doing what is often a time consuming task and possibly a tedious one.

The basic idea is that when a person normally writes something, they almost always have to look things up and then write about them. If the needed information is peripheral to the main subject on which the author is writing, you have to find the information before you can include it. With Generative AI, the process of writing is better and faster. Information that would ordinarily be impossible to obtain is now available.

The process uses a generative transformer named ChatGPT that is readily available to all users. The process is called *easy writing*.

How does this easy writing work? The author gets an idea and delineates the areas for which he needs information. He or she sends a request in the form of a query to ChatGTP, and then the software returns the answer. The author then combines the various forms of information to construct whatever the original idea entails. It's that simple. It's your story or report or message or request so you can use the generated information in any way you desire. In this book, the title of each chapter is the subject for the query and the following text is the book chapter generated by generative computing.

As far as this book is concerned —you are reading – you may copy it in whole or in part and distribute it is any form you wish. If you change it, please take my name off of it. There is only one limitation. You can't sell it. How would I know? To make money, you need distribution.

The book in which this short note is contained was written with the help of AI. More specifically, I used ChatGPT. I chose *strategy* as the main topic. It is a subject that I knew something about, but not very much. The content is useful and many persons can benefit from reading it. There is also information on Singularity, AI Ontology, ELIZA, and the Turing Test, all a part of AI.

Each and every chapter was written using the AI system. I am going to refer to it as *Chat*. My only contribution was the selection of subjects and cleaning up the various Chat entries. A typical query to Chat is "What is Service Strategy." You will get a relevant response, and I guarantee you that Chat was not an English major.

The author's job is to select the overall subject matter, as is the subject 'strategy' in this case, as well as 'artificial intelligence' in the second part of the book. The author's second job is to perform a copy editing of the subject matter. By looking at the subject matter, you will see some corrected text and some that was not corrected. Some uncorrected text is included to give an idea of what has to be done.

Chat performs the research for you, and that is the idea of what 'A computer written book' is all about. Perhaps in the future, AI will select the subject matter and the various topics.

ABOUT THE AUTHOR

Harry Katzan, Jr. is a professor who has written several books and many papers on computers and service science. He has been an advisor to the executive board of a major bank and a general consultant on various disciplines. He and his wife have lived in Switzerland where he was a banking consultant and a visiting professor of Artificial Intelligence. He is an avid runner and has completed 94 marathons including Boston 13 times and New York 14 times. He holds bachelors, masters, and doctorate degrees.

RELEVANT BOOKS BY HARRY KATZAN JR.

Lessons in Artificial Intelligence
Artificial Intelligence A Primer
Artificial Intelligence Concepts for Management
Artificial Intelligence Theory for Management
Artificial Intelligence Ontology for Management
Management of Artificial Intelligence
Artificial Intelligence Novel
On the Trail of Artificial Intelligence
Advanced Lessons for Artificial Intelligence
Conspectus of Artificial Intelligence
Artificial Intelligence is a Service
The K-REPORT
Strategy and AI